# Untranslatable Song:

## A
Selection
of
the
Vertical
Poetry
of
Roberto Juarroz

translated
by

**Wally Swist**

FIRST INTERNATIONAL EDITION, April 2026
Library of Congress Control Number: *pending*
ISBN 978-1-965784-51-8 HARDBACK
ISBN 978-1-965784-50-1 PAPERBACK
Printed in the United States of America, Canada, Australia,
Saudi Arabia, Japan, India, Brazil, and the European Union.

Book Typography & Graphic Design by Kurt Lovelace
Cover type *Bauhaus Dessau* **Alfarn** by Céline Hurka,
Elia Preuss, Flavia Zimbardi,
Hidetaka Yamasaki, and Luca Pellegrini.
Author name, blurbs, footers in **Jenson** by Robert Slimbach.
Back cover description in **Gill Sans Nova**.
Titles and body text set in **Baskerville**.
Flourishes set in Emigre Foundry **Dalliance** by Frank Heine.
Emigre Foundry **ZeitGuys** by Bob Aufuldish, Eric Donelan.
Typefaces licensed Adobe, Linotype, Emigre, & URW GmbH.

PierianSpringsPress.Com
PIERIAN SPRINGS PRESS, INC
30 N GOULD ST, STE 25398
SHERIDAN, WYOMING 82801-6317

For Tevis Kimball

And The Readers
Of These Translations

# CONTENTS

# FOREWORD

KURT LOVELACE

To open a book of Roberto Juarroz is to feel the floor tilt, but very, very quietly.

So much in these poems looks almost harmless at first glance: a thread, a bell, a fly on the ceiling, a blank page, a tree, a stone. The language is spare, nearly didactic in its simplicity, and yet the effect is a slow, lucid vertigo. Juarroz called what he wrote poesía vertical, vertical poetry, because each poem does not so much move forward in time as "drop" into the depth of an instant, an object, a word, or a void.

What Wally Swist has accomplished in Untranslatable Song is, in that sense, doubly vertical. These are poems that already move along an inner axis, from surface to depth, from the visible to what he calls "the bottom of things", and Swist must somehow reproduce that descent in English, a language that is often more literal, less hospitable to abstraction, and suspicious of aphorism. The result, in this collection, is a conversation between two styles of plainness: Juarroz's austere, metaphysical Spanish and Swist's persevering English.

As a translator myself, I read this book not only as a lover of Juarroz's work, but as a colleague listening closely to the decisions another translator has made: where to stay literal, where to risk idiom, where to let the Spanish strangeness stand and where to naturalize it into English.

# THE VERTICAL GESTURE:
## WHAT THESE POEMS ARE DOING

The selection Swist offers moves more or less chronologically, from early poems in Primera poesía vertical (1958) through passages in the Eleventh Poesía vertical (1988). We watch Juarroz refine the same fundamental obsessions over three decades:

- What is "the bottom of things"?
- How do life and death interpenetrate?
- What is the status of words, silence, and the blank page?
- What happens when time folds on itself and the self meets its other versions?
- How does a human being become "real", a man, a lover, a mortal, through gestures that may not even be his own?

Already in I.4, Juarroz insists that "the bottom of things is not life or death" (el fondo de las cosas no es la vida o la muerte). Instead, something else is waiting "to come to the shore." The poem offers a series of surreal, lucid images, a kind of metaphysical testimony, that prove this to him: air that "goes barefoot" in birds, a "roof of absences" that shelters silence, a gaze that turns itself around at the very bottom of perception. Childhood becomes "bread before flour," a stunning image of pre-formation, of meaning existing before material.

The gesture is typical: Juarroz moves from statement to image to statement again. The poem does not argue; it offers a series of metaphors as evidence, almost like experimental data for a metaphysics of depth.

Over the course of the book we see him return to this movement again and again:

- In II.23, after "half a life or maybe all of it," only certain tremblings resist oblivion: a place "where parallels tremble," a night when a dead love lives again, strange fidelities that allow us to "postpone a little the impossibility of everything."

- In V.1, he speaks of "the root of the word" as a place where love plays and also discovers its limitation. After language, at its root, a "space without passion or sarcasm" opens, cleared ground where a more human absence can grow.
- In VIII (1984), he counsels that we must periodically abandon writing to live with the blank page, its too-smooth plain, its too-open horizon, so as to approach not our imaginations, but our "transfigurations."

These are poems of procedures of thought. They are little operations on reality, "what happens if we turn the eyes backward," "what happens if it rains onto thought," "what happens if silence is treated as a temple without a god." They are philosophical experiments couched in the simplest possible language.

Swist's translations, characteristically, follow the structure and lineation closely. He keeps Juarroz's sober tone, resisting the temptation to embellish. At their best, his English versions feel like clear glass over a strange architecture. At their roughest, they sound like someone thinking in Spanish through the medium of English, a quality that is not always a fault in this kind of metaphysical poetry, but sometimes muddies the clarity of the original.

## A World Built of Simple Things

One of the first surprises of Juarroz's work is that these highly abstract, philosophical poems are almost always built from extremely concrete, almost childish objects: trees, nests, bells, birds, threads, rings, hands, lines, notes, clouds, clods of earth.

Think of the great poem IV.1, where life and death draw the same basic figures, tree, nest, bird, and an invisible "hand that draws nothing" rearranges them, sometimes erasing one part of the series, sometimes doubling another. At the end, in one version, a single bird inhabits "one nest on the tree of life and the tree of death."

This is a model for much of the collection:

- Tree / nest / bird become interchangeable units in an algebra of life and death.
- A "hand that does not draw anything" stands for a force beyond our representational power: fate, chance, God, or sheer alterity.
- The poem moves through simple permutations of the same few elements until it reaches a configuration in which "nothing is missing or left over."

Swist's English here is remarkably clean. The central triad, "life draws a tree / and death draws another. / Life draws a nest / and death copies it", retains the almost childlike clarity of the Spanish. Where the original says una mano que no dibuja nada ("a hand that draws nothing"), Swist's "a hand that does not draw anything" maintains the almost fussy literalness Juarroz likes. This is a case where too much idiom, "an invisible hand," say, would have betrayed a key strangeness: the insistence on drawing and not-drawing as the very axis of the poem.

The same pattern recurs in other poems:

- VI.4: the bell is "full of wind," the bird "full of flight," the word "full of voice," even when nothing seems to be happening. All things are said to "flee toward their presence", a marvelous metaphysical inversion.
- VII.4: a bell sounding "from below everything" serves no practical purpose, no temple, no springtime, no funeral. It rings "like a natural movement" as if, at the bottom of things, there were nothing but a detached pealing.
- II.21: people depart "as best they can," some with their ID in their pocket, others with their moon "screwed into their blood," others with nothing at all. And yet all "leave with their feet tied," along paths they took, paths

they didn't, and paths they will never take.

The power of these poems lies in a double motion: the objects are utterly ordinary, but the logical operations performed on them are startling. Bells and birds and ID cards become tools for thinking about death, presence, and the impossibility of completion.

As a translator, Swist is generally wise to maintain the ordinary tone of the objects. He doesn't upgrade terrón to "clod of earth" when "clod" alone will do; he keeps "ID card" for cédula de identidad, letting the bureaucratic note sound. Occasionally, though, his English treats the object too roughly, and something delicate is lost, for instance, allowing "air" to behave somewhat less smoothly in English than the mystery that pervades the Spanish.

## Metaphor, Image, and the Logic of the Impossible

Juarroz works with metaphors that are both transparent and impossible. Many of them are stated without connective tissue; they sit in the poem like axioms.

Some characteristic types in this selection include the following.

### Reversed Causality And Inside-Outness

- "It rains onto thought; and thought rains over the world."
- Thought rains inside the world, then under the world, then "without" the world, and yet it keeps raining.
- In another poem, "the lightning of beauty" creates eternity on the back side of the eye; "the lightning of the instant" creates eternity on the far side of time.

These metaphors operate almost as logical functions: if light has a front, then eternity must be on its reverse; if rain falls on the world, what happens when we treat thought as the sky above it?

## Self-Divided Subjectivity

- In I.13, the speaker's hands work without him while he sleeps and may be the ones "making" him into a man; when they finish, they will wake him and "show him" the man he has become.
- In III.9, he runs a "race with the one I was and the one I will be" and then imagines a third race in which he is "passed" by something or someone else: that, he says, will be the real race.
- In I.29, he turns his eyes "backward" and dies "behind himself," of "no-god and no-someone."

3. Almost-scholastic abstractions given concrete anchors

- A "hum in the background" that accuses the presence of things, then their absence, then the possibility that there is nothing that cannot exist. Each phase requires a different human response: words and wind, an invented memory, a "silence doubled from silence."
- Silence as "a temple that does not need god."
- A blank page whose too-smooth plain and too-open horizon become places we must learn to inhabit.

The logic is rigorous but not discursive. Juarroz is constantly trying to build metaphysical structures out of these metaphorical moves.

Swist's English generally follows the metaphors closely, sometimes at the expense of idiomatic flow. For instance, in IV.6, Juarroz's "Llueve sobre el pensamiento" becomes "It rains onto thought", a choice that preserves the literal preposition sobre as "onto," which is slightly odd in English, but not fatally so. As the poem proceeds, "It rains inside thought," "It rains under thought", the repetition of "rains" and the prepositions produce a kind of incantatory logic, which Swist wisely preserves line for line.

In other poems, especially those with more philosophical

vocabulary, the English tips toward Latinate abstraction in a way that feels natural to Juarroz's style: instancia, gradaciones, imposibilidad, fidelidades all have close English cognates. The danger, however, is that English grows heavy with stacked abstractions more quickly than Spanish does. A translator has to decide, sometimes line by line, how much weight the English sentence can bear before the image collapses. Swist mostly allows the abstraction to stand, perhaps trusting the reader's ear for philosophy.

### Puns, Wordplay, and Cultural Nuances

Spanish is a language rich in semantic density and homonymic suggestion; Juarroz, though not a punster in the obvious sense, often depends on fields of meaning that English splits apart.

A few recurring knots:

1. Fondo, bottom, depth, background, ground

In I.4 and again in VII.4, fondo carries several senses at once:

- The "bottom" of things (metaphysical depth)
- The background or underlying hum of reality
- The bottom of a well, the depth of the world, the innermost part of a bell's ring

Swist translates el fondo de las cosas as "the bottom of things," which is accurate but slightly spatially flat. "The depths of things" or "the ground of things" would emphasize metaphysical depth rather than mere underside. Later, in the bell poem, he speaks of "the bottom of everything," which works better in English, hinting at both metaphysical ground and simple "down below." The ambiguity is not entirely recoverable; fondo resonates philosophically in Spanish (think of el fondo del asunto, "the heart of the matter"), while in English "bottom" is more prosaic and "depth" more solemn. A translator must pick one at each occurrence; Swist tends toward "bottom," and the reader is left to infer the rest.

### 2. Hilo and punto, thread, point

In II.18, the thread that unites two people's eyes when they are not looking at each other is "más delgada que el pensamiento", "thinner than thought." It has a "gauge of nothing" (calibre de nada), supporting an idea that just barely exists. In IV.7, punto (point) becomes the site where something breaks, where two deaths approach each other, where something "will always be that something." The poems riff on the mathematical, emotional, and metaphysical senses of "point," including "point in time" and "point of contact."

English can follow punto fairly well; "point" carries many of the same meanings. With hilo, however, some nuance vanishes. Spanish hears hilar (to spin) and hilación (threading, coherence) in the background; a thread is also the logic that holds things together. "Thread" in English has a similar metaphoric sense ("thread of argument"), so Swist's choice here is apt. Where I might tweak is in "thread with a gauge of nothing," which is literal but mechanical. Perhaps "a thread as fine as nothing at all" would keep the paradox while softening the technicality.

### 3. Sonar / taner, to sound / to ring

In VII.4, the bell "sounds from below everything" (suena desde abajo de todo). Swist renders taner, a more archaic verb for playing a bell, as "ringing in total detachment," which is a thoughtful solution. The original's distinction between sonar and tañer (a deliberate, almost liturgical action) is hard to mirror; English has only "to ring," "to chime," "to toll." But his phrase "in total detachment" effectively reintroduces the nuance of disinterested action that tañer suggests.

### 4. Olvido, forgetting, oblivion

In VII.17 and elsewhere, olvido is both a common noun ("forgetfulness") and a nearly mythic, almost proper name for oblivion. Swist keeps "oblivion" in at least one key instance, which is wise; "forgetfulness" would sound too psychological, too small. At the same time, where a phrase like "la palabra olvido" appears, there is an almost comical literalness in "the word oblivion" that English readers may find heavier than Spanish ones. There is no perfect solution; one lives with the slight over-weighting of the term.

### 5. Cultural textures

Juarroz is less culturally localized than many Latin American poets; his world is abstract, almost placeless. Still, some details carry specifically Latin American or Argentine resonances:

- The cédula de identidad in II.21 evokes the bureaucratic state, familiar throughout the Southern Cone.
- Childhood as "bread before flour" conjures a culture where bread is daily and emblematic.
- References to Octavio Paz and Paul Éluard situate the poet in a specific international modernist conversation.

Swist tends to keep these references intact, not domesticating them. This is the right choice; Juarroz is already oddly "un-national" in his imagery, and the few specifically Latin American details should remain visible as anchors.

### Particular Translation Questions

It may be helpful now to look at a few specific translation choices that shape the reader's experience, both where Swist's solutions shine and where slightly different English might better serve Juarroz's intention.

1. I.4, "The bottom of things is not life or death."

The opening poem sets the tone for the whole selection. Swist's first line, "The bottom of things is not life or death," is very close to "El fondo de las cosas no es la vida o la muerte." The choice of "bottom" is defensible, but, as I suggested, "The depths of things are neither life nor death" might more clearly signal that we're dealing with metaphysical depth, not just underside.

Later in the poem, "el aire que se descalza en los pájaros" becomes "the air is barefoot in the birds." This is literal enough, but in Spanish descalzarse is an action: to take off one's shoes. I hear something like "the air takes off its shoes in the birds," or, a bit more fluid: "the air goes barefoot in the birds." Swist's "is barefoot" feels slightly static, less playful.

More problematic is the clause about childhood: "Y también me lo prueba / mi niñez..." Swist gives us "And I also tried it / on my childhood that was bread before flour." The Spanish clearly means "And my childhood also proves it to me", childhood is another witness, not an object of experiment. A more faithful line might read:

> "And my childhood proves it to me as well,
>     my childhood that was bread before flour..."

This preserves the logic: these images "prove" that the bottom of things is something other than life or death.

Near the end, "papeles donde el hombre está inmóvil" is rendered as "parts where a man is motionless." Here Swist seems to have misread papeles as "parts" (roles), but Juarroz almost surely means "papers" or "pages", places where a human figure is fixed as writing or text. "Pages where man is motionless" would better retain the latent self-reflexivity of the poem: the poet himself is writing on pages as he says this.

2. I.13, "Sometimes my hands awaken me."

This is one of the most beautiful poems in the selection.

Swist's opening, "Sometimes my hands awaken me. / They make or break something without me, / while I sleep", follows the original closely and captures its quiet eeriness.

Later, though, a small but telling ambiguity arises. "Y no sé hacer un hombre." This can mean "I do not know how to make a man" (to form a person) or "I do not know how to be a man." Given the rest of the poem, where the hands may be forming the speaker as he sleeps, the creative sense seems truer. Swist's "And I don't know how to become a man" leans toward personal development, which is legitimate but slightly narrows the verse. I might prefer:

> "And I don't know how to make a man."

which keeps open the possibility that the hands are craftsmen, not just midwives of identity.

### 3. I.22, The voice that wakes us

"No debería ser posible / dormirse sin tener cerca / una voz para poderse despertar." Swist: "It shouldn't be possible / to fall asleep without being nearby you / a voice to awaken to." The meaning is clear, but "being nearby you a voice" is not idiomatic English. A smoother rendering that keeps the Juarroz simplicity might be:

> "It shouldn't be possible
>   to fall asleep without having near us
>   a voice to wake to."

Similarly, the second stanza's emphasis on "one's own voice" is key: you should not fall asleep without having your own voice near, to wake you. This hints at an inner prompting, a self that calls us back from oblivion.

### 4. I.25, "A day will come"

The poem about the "great union" imagines a future when we no longer have to push glass to make it fall or hammer nails to make them hold. Swist's "to push the glass to make it fall" is faithful but slightly awkward; "to shove the panes so they'll fall" or "to knock at the glass to make it break" would introduce more concrete imagery. Juarroz uses vidrios (panes, glass shards), which already conveys a sense of fragility.

"Even God will learn to speak" is an excellent, stark choice for "Hasta Dios aprenderá a hablar", preserving both the humor and the scandal. Later, the translator keeps the sensuality in "The stones will be like your breasts," and "I will make my verses with my hands, / so that no one can be confused anymore" nicely catches the tactile insistence of hacer los versos con las manos, poetry as manual work, not mere voice.

### 5. IV.2, Walking upside down, walking "head up"

In the poem dedicated to Paul Éluard, a fly on the ceiling, a man in the street, and a god in nothingness all "go head-down." Only "you" are not walking, unless pure absences invent a new way of walking: "walking head up." Swist keeps this literal, "walking head up", which is correct, if odd. One might be tempted to say "upright," but that would soften the delightfully blunt image of a head turned the right way.

Elsewhere in the poem, however, Swist's English becomes slightly tangled: "let's explore the meeting of love and stone, / the journey hand in hand to your grief..." where the original speaks of "el viaje de la mano a su duelo" (the journey of the hand to its own mourning). The difference is subtle: Juarroz's line hints at the hand's autonomous grief; the English pulls it more into the general human "your grief." Given the poem's interest in bodies and orientations, I would keep the hand as subject: "the journey of the hand toward its mourning."

### 6. VIII, The blank page

The brief lyric about abandoning writing to coexist with

the blank page is almost proverbially clear in Spanish. Swist renders "la página en blanco" as "the blank page" and "su llanura demasiado lisa" as "its too smooth plainness," which is faithful if slightly padded by "plainness" after "plain." I might suggest "its plain that is too smooth" to maintain a physical image of a flat field, not just abstract plainness.

More puzzling is "dialogue with them at the end of the target," where the original has "en el extremo del blanco", literally, "at the edge of the blank/whiteness." "Target" seems to be a mistranslation; perhaps an autocorrect from "blank" or a mistaken association with a shooting target. To keep the sense of limit, I would say "at the edge of the blankness" or "at the far edge of the whiteness."


## Silence, Absence, and the Sacred

One of the most impressive strands running through Untranslatable Song is Juarroz's insistent thinking about silence, speech, and the divine. Several poems here function almost as small treatises.

VII.17, for instance, declares that "every silence is a magical space," containing a hidden rite, a gestating word, and some small point of "anti-silence", a clod striking the earth, a trickle of water through the world's dream, the sound of a hand knocking from inside a poem. The conclusion, "Silence is a temple / that does not need god", is one of Juarroz's exemplary aphorisms, at once religious and secular. Swist keeps it nearly literal, including the lower-case "god," which leans into the philosophical rather than confessional register.

In V.1, at "the root of the word," various loves play, but they return with a "recklessly dark flower," acknowledging that they cannot go any further. After the word, at its root, opens a passionless space in which the most human absence can grow freely. This is a theology of language: words do not save us, but they clear a place for our most honest absence to stand.

In the dream-poem from Eleventh Vertical Poetry, the poet dreams of a manuscript whose lines erase themselves, along with its authors, until only one line is left, itself beginning to vanish: "Only God can save you from God." Swist's English here is strong and stark; the rhythm is good, and the line arrives with the right mixture of terror and resignation. It encapsulates one of Juarroz's core fears and insights: that whatever we imagine as ultimate may itself be ambivalent, dangerous, and that only something beyond that, another God, another depth of being, could rescue us.

Throughout, Swist's tone for these quasi-theological statements is admirably restrained. He does not italicize, dramatize, or decorate. He simply lays out the sentences and trusts Juarroz's thought to do the work. Where small infelicities of English occur, odd prepositions, slightly off verbs, they generally don't obscure the theological line; they are more noticeable in the earlier, more narrative poems than in these terse, meditative ones.

### "UNTRANSLATABLE SONG"

The titular poem of the collection, VII.1, gives us the image that Swist has wisely chosen to stand for the whole book:

> Use your own hand as a pillow,
> the sky with its clouds,
> the earth with its clods,
> the falling tree with its foliage...

Only then, Juarroz says, can we hear the "song without distance," the song that does not enter the ear because it is already there, the only song that does not repeat. And he ends: "Every person needs an untranslatable song."

The Spanish is as plain as the English here; the phrase

"una canción intraducible" is almost shockingly simple after so much metaphysical elaboration. Swist keeps it literal. There is no better phrase than "untranslatable song" in English; "unsayable" or "inexpressible" would weaken the concreteness. It is not that we lack words; it is that we each need one song so intimate, so structurally ours, that translation, even into another human's understanding, would distort it.

The irony, of course, is that we encounter this idea through translation. A poem that declares the necessity of something untranslatable appears in a bilingual edition, in a project that depends on the belief that enough can cross the gap to justify the attempt. That irony is productive; it's part of what gives this collection its charm and gravity.

Swist's versions, absent occasional roughness, keep the essential features of Juarroz's style:

- The short, assertive sentences that open into paradox.
- The simple, elemental images: bell, thread, blank page, tree, nest, bird.
- The movement from statement to image to re-statement that characterizes his thought.

Where I've suggested alternative wordings, they are meant less as corrections than as footnotes from a fellow traveler. Translating Juarroz is not a matter of polishing awkward English into smooth idiom; it is a matter of deciding, poem by poem, which kind of strangeness you are willing to accept. A too-smooth version would betray the underlying difficulty and risk of the original; a too-literal one can obscure moments of sharp, crystalline clarity.

This collection, happily, leans toward fidelity to that difficulty. Swist lets Juarroz's peculiar stance, the almost childlike voice speaking severe metaphysics, remain visible. Sometimes we hear the Spanish breathing just beneath the English, and I would argue that this, too, is a form of "untranslatable song": the residue of another language inside our own.

As you read these poems, in both versions if you can, you participate in their vertical movement. You move from the ordinary to the impossible, from the blank page to the space beyond words, from the hum in the background to the moment when, "on any given afternoon, a bird comes to perch in the air as if the air were another branch", and then all the humming stops.

It is in that paused instant, I think, that the true work of this book happens: not in Spanish or in English, but in the small, unmarked space where the two briefly coincide, and then fall silent.

**Kurt Lovelace,** author of
*Halfway Between Everywhere*
**Friday 17 October 2025**

## Untranslatable Song:
## The Vertical Poetry of Roberto Juarroz

*Ir hacia arriba no es nada mas*
*que un poco mas corto o un poco*
*mas largo que ir hacia abajo*

Going up is nothing more
that a little shorter or a little
longer than going down

The allusion to "Fragment 108" of Heraclitus is significant to the poetry of Roberto Juarroz. It exhibits his predilection toward a philosophical and lyrical tautology in his poetry but also the mysterious *something,* or ontological underpinning, Juarroz either aspires to or characteristically drills down toward. His poetical *raison d'etre* is best explained, perhaps, in a letter to W. S. Merwin, dated 26 August 1986.

*My father died in my arms, of lung cancer, and I breathed death. I turned away from the church and its splendors, but I was tinged with something approaching mysticism, which in that non-confessional, primal, and open sense of which Novalis was speaking when he described poetry as the original religion of humanity.*

For a poet who is also considered to be an aphorist, and who was a friend and colleague of Antonio Porchia, a master of the form, the poetry of Juarroz is more substantive than what is an oversimplification of his style and form. The essence of aphorism may be apparent in the work of Juarroz but he is much similar in nature to the work of Polish poet Tadeusz Rosewicz, or as Julio Cortazar suggested to Mallarme, due to his "use of absence." Perhaps even Emily Dickinson's notion of poetry being "written at a slant" would also afford Juarroz a certain verisimilitude in describing the kind of poetry he composed.

His own words, again, may be the most felicitous in who Juarroz is and was as a poet, again from the letter quoted above.

*I know that I have written something relatively different. I am not
Interested in literary success nor in being rich, nor in the socio-
literary farce. I want something open and clear. I keep a few great
admirations (Porchia, for example, and Rilke and Huidobro). I have
always had a number of close friends; man matters deeply to me;
I am a little startled by this growing recognition in recent year, and
the voices that reach me from many directions; but I have a profound
faith in something that I can only intimate in my poems,
and I would like to live a little longer.*

Roberto Juarroz was born in 1925 in Coronel Dorrego, near Buenos Aires, in Argentina. He died in his seventieth year in the early spring of 1995. He developed a passion for poetry early on and published his first iteration of *Vertical Poesies* in 1958, of which not unlike Antonio Porchia with his *Voces*, would continue to publish poems without titles in volumes that would be issued by the same name, *Vertical Poetry,* only differing by their successive numbers identifying each book's new work.

Octavio Paz wrote of the poetry of Juarroz that he saw it as "surprising verbal crystallisation; language reduced to a bead of light." In returning to the notion of a philosophical arc informing his poetry, Andreas Dorschel praises Juarroz for writing "philosophical poetry," which he concludes is "transparent and dark at the same time, marked by "its lightness and metaphysical wit."

Perhaps this is best displayed in one of my own favorite poems written by Roberto Juarroz, one dedicated to his wife, Laura Cerrato, who would provide the impetus to publish the fifteenth iteration of *Vertical Poetry* after the death of her husband, which appeared in 1997. Juarroz referred to Laura as his "irreplaceable companion."

**Vertical Poetry, IV, 7, 1969**

*Si conocieram0s el punto*
*donde va a romperse algo,*
*donde se cortara el hilo do los besos,*
*donde una mirada dejara de encontrarse con otra mirada,*
*donde el corazon saltara hacia otro sitio,*
*podriamos poner otro punto sobre ese punto*
*o por lo menos acompanarlo al romperse.*

*Si conocieramos el punto*
*donde algo va a fundirse con algo,*
*donde el desierto se encontrara con la lluvia,*
*donde el abrazo se tocara con la vida,*
*donde mi muerte se aproximara a la tuya,*
*podriamos desenvolver ese punto como una serpentina*
*o por lo menos cantarlo hasta morirnos.*

*Si concieramos el punto*
*donde algo sera siempre ese algo,*
*donde el hueso no olivdara a la carne,*
*donde la fuente es madre de otra fuente,*
*donde el pasado dejar solo ese punto y borrar todos los otros*
*o guardarlo por lo menos en un lugar mas seguro.*

*(A Laura)*

If we knew the point
where something is going to break,
where the thread of kisses will be cut,
where one look would stop meeting another look,
where the heart will jump to another place,
we could put another point on that point.
or at least accompany it when it breaks.

If we knew the point
where something is going to merge with something,
where the desert met the rain,
where the hug touched life,
where my death would approach yours,
we could unwrap that song like a streamer
or at least sing it until we die.

If we knew the point
where something will always be that something,
where the bone will not forget the flesh,
where the source is the mother of another source,
where the past leaves only that point and erases all the others
or store it at least in a safer place.

(*To Laura*)

I first read Roberto Juarroz in 1977 when I was a cataloguer in an all-poetry bookstore in New Haven, Connecticut. The volume was just entitled *Vertical Poetry,* a bilingual edition translated by W. S. Merwin and published by the inimitable Kayak Books. I carried that book around with me on long walks through the city and through Yale campus, often reciting verses quietly to myself that I learned by heart. I also would open readings I gave then in various lofts with any number of my favorite translations from that book. The music of the poems of Roberto Juarroz, which is not much discussed at all, penetrated my inner ear and remained there. The best I can describe it is a forefront of violins against a backdrop of sonic harmonies: a kind of infinite music or maybe even a music of infinity, but one that is humble and nourishing concomitantly.

Librarian, university professor, and poet, Roberto Juarroz is a name not necessarily known in many literary contexts and conversations, but neither is humor or transparency for that matter, since there are elements of humor, a sophisticated kind, and many layers of transparencies in the poetry of Juarroz. Juarroz even suggests, perhaps assuming his role as professor, which he held at the University of Buenos Aires, that maybe the best poem was unwritten, and in doing so this could be the beginning of understanding the source from which all great writing not only begins but whence it continues to flourish.

**Vertical Poetry, VIII, 1984**

*Hay que empezar a abandonar cada tanto la escritura*
*y aprender a convivir con la pagina en blanco,*
*con su llanura desmasiado lisa,*
*con su horizonte demansiado abierto.*

*Hay que dejar en suspenso nuestras figuraciones*
*para aproximarnos a nuestras transfiguraciones*
*y dialogar con ellas en el extremo del blanco,*
*sin tener siquiera la letra como testigo.*

You have to start abandoning writing from time to time
and learn to live with the blank page,
with its too smooth plainness,
with its horizon too open.

We must leave our imaginations in suspense
to approach our transfigurations
and dialogue with them at the end of the target,
without even having the handwriting as a witness.

The reference made by Julio Cortazar to the poetry of
Roberto Juarroz is quite apt regarding Juarroz's penchant for
representing "absences;" or what we experience when we exact
true presence in our lives, as in deep meditation, and most
certainly in the following poem, since when I attempt to
describe the music in the poetry of Roberto Juarroz as a
forefront of violins and a background of lyric harmonies,
undeniably, it is his "untranslatable song."

**Vertical Poetry, 7.1, 1982**

*Usar la propia mano como almohada.*
*El cielo lo hace con sus nubes,*
*la tierra con sus terrones*
*y el arbol que cae*
*con su propio follaje.*

*Solo asi puede escucharse*
*la cancion sin distancia,*
*la cancion que no entra en el oido*
*porque esta en el oido,*
*la unica cancion que no se repite.*

*Todo hombre necesita
una cancion intraducible.*

Use your own hand as a pillow.
Sky does it with its clouds,
earth with its clods
and the tree that falls
with its own foliage.

Only then can the song
without distance be heard,
the song that never enters the ear
because it's already in the ear,
the only song that is not repeated.

All people need
an untranslatable song.

# Untranslatable Song:

## A
## Selection
## of
## the
## Vertical
## Poetry
## of
## Roberto Juarroz

*Vertical Poetry, I.4, 1958*

*El fondo de las cosas no es la vida o la muerte.*
*Me lo prueban*
*el aire que se descalza en los parjaros,*
*un tejado de ausencias que acomoda el silencio,*
*y esta mirada mia que se da vuelta en el fondo,*
*como todas las cosas se dan vuelta cuando acaban.*

*Y tambien me lo preuba*
*mi ninez que era pan anterior a la harina,*
*mi ninez que sabia*
*que hay humos que descienden,*
*voces con las que nadie habla,*
*papeles donde el hombre esta inmovil.*

*El fondo de las cosas no es la muerte o la vida.*
*El fondo es otra cosa*
*que alguna vez sale a la orilla.*

The bottom of things is not life or death.
It is proven to me
that the air is barefoot in the birds,
the roof of absences that accommodates silence,
and this look of mine that turns in the background,
like all things turn around when they end.

And I also tried it
on my childhood that was bread before flour,
my childhood that I knew
that there is smoke that descends,
voices with which no one speaks,
papers where a man is motionless.

The bottom of things is not life or death.
The background is something else
that ever comes to the shore.

*Vertical Poetry, I.13, 1958*

*A veces mis manos me despiertan.*
*Ellas hacen o deshacen algo sin mi,*
*mientras yo duermo,*
*algo terriblemente humano,*
*concreto como la espalda o el bolsillo de un hombre.*

*Las oigo desde el sueno*
*en su labor afuera,*
*pero al abrir los ojos ya estan quietas.*
*Sin embargo,*
*he pensado que tal vez yo sea hombre*
*por eso que ellas hacen*
*con su gesto y no el mio,*
*con su Dios y no el mio,*
*con su muerte, si tambien ellas mueren.*

*Y no se hacer un hombre.*
*Tal vez lo hagan mis manos mientras duermo*
*y cuando este acabado*
*me despierten del todo*
*y me lo muestren.*

Sometimes my hands awaken me.
They make or break something without me,
while I sleep,
something terribly human,
concrete like a back or pocket of a man.

I hear them from sleep
in their work outside,
but when you open your eyes they are already still.
Nevertheless,
I thought that maybe I am a man
because of what they do
with their gesture and not mine,
with their God and not mine,
with their death, it they also die.

And I don't know how to become a man.
Maybe my hands do it while I sleep
and when its finished
wake me up completely
and show it to me.

*Vertical Poetry, I.22, 1958*


*No deberia ser posible*
*dormirse sin tener cerca*
*una voz para poderse despertar.*

*No debiera ser posible*
*dormirse sin tener cerca*
*la propia voz para poderse despertar.*

*No debiera ser posible*
*dormirse sin despertar*
*en el momento justo en que el sueno se encuentra*
*con esos ojos abiertos*
*que ya no necesitan dormir mas.*

It shouldn't be possible
to fall asleep without being nearby you
a voice to awaken to.

It shouldn't be possible
falling asleep without being nearby
one's own voice to awaken.

It shouldn't be possible
to fall asleep without waking
at the right moment in which the dream is found
with those eyes open
that don't need to sleep anymore.

*Vertical Poetry, I.25, 1958*

*Llegara un dia*
*en el cual no habra que empujar los vidrios para que caigan,*
*ni martillar los clavos para que sostengan,*
*ni posar las piedras para que se callen.*

*Empezara la gran union.*
*Hasta Dios aprendera a hablar*
*y el aire y la luz*
*entraran en su cueva de miedosas enternidades.*

*Entonces ya no habra diferencia entre tus ojos y tu vientre,*
*ni entre mis palabras y mi voz.*
*Las piedras seran como tus senos*
*y yo hare mis versos con las manos,*
*para que nadie pueda ya confundirse.*

A day will come
in which there would be no need to push the glass
        to make it fall,
nor hammer the nails to hold them,
nor put the stones to rest so that they remain silent.

The great union will begin.
Even God will learn to speak
and the air and the light
will enter their cave of fearful enternities.

Then there will be no difference between your eyes
        and your belly,
nor between my words and my voice.
The stones will be like your breasts
and I will make my verses with my hands,
so that no one can be confused anymore.

*Vertical Poetry, I.26, 1958*


*Mi rostro me esta mirando desde el polvo.*

*Yo no desde donde los miro,*
*pero entre ambos crece como un telon en ruinas*
*la distancia desnuda,*
*la distancia que nadie ocupara.*

My face is looking at me from the dust.

Not from where I look at them,
but between them it grows like a ruined curtain
the naked distance,
the distance that no one will occupy.

*Vertical Poetry, I.29, 1958*


*Pongo los ojos hacia atras,*
*como alguna vez puse a dios hacia adelante*
*o el tacto pensativo con que he amado.*

*Y como alguna vez no puse nada,*
*ni adelante ni atras,*
*puse mi sombra*
*o quiza la de algo que no encuentro.*

*Pongo los ojos hacia atras*
*u me muero atras mio,*
*me muero de no dios y de no alguien.*

*Sera la juerto acaso*
*un puro ir hacia atras,*
*un irse atras sin nadie?*

I roll back my eyes,
as I ever put God forward
or the thoughtful touch with which I have loved.

And since once I didn't place anything,
either forward or backward,
I place my shadow
or maybe something I can't find.

I roll back my eyes
and I'm dying behind me,
I am dying of no god and no one.

Maybe it will be the right one
a pure going backwards,
to leave behind without anyone?

*Vertical Poetry, II.18, 1963*

*Una hebra mas delgada que el pensamiento,*
*un hilo con calibre de nada,*
*une nuestros ojos cuando no nos miramos.*

*Cuando nos miramos*
*nos unen todos los hilos del mundo,*
*pero falta este,*
*que solo da sombra*
*a la luz mas secreta del amor.*

*Despues que nos vayamos,*
*quiza quede este hilo*
*uniendo nuestros sitios vacios.*

A thread thinner than thought,
a thread with a gauge of nothing,
unites our eyes when they are no looking at each other.

When we look at each other
all the threads of the world unite us,
but this one is missing,
that only gives shadow
to the most secret light of love.

After we leave,
maybe this thread remains
uniting our empty places.

*Vertical Poetry, II.21, 1963*

*Cada uno se va como puede,*
*unos con el pecho entreabierto,*
*otros con una sola mano,*
*unos con la cedula de identidad en el bolsillo,*
*otras en el alma,*
*unos con la luna atornillada en la sangre*
*y otros sin sangre, ni luna, ni recuerdos.*

*Cada uno se va aunque se va,*
*unos con el amor entre dientes,*
*otros cambiandose la piel,*
*unos con la vida y la muerte,*
*otros con la muerte y la vida,*
*unos con la manos en su hombre*
*y otros en el hombro de otro.*

*Cada uno se va porque se va,*
*unos con alguien trasnochado entre las cejas,*
*otros sin haberse cruzado con nadie,*
*unos por la puerta que da o parece da sobre el camino,*
*otros por una puerta dibujada en la pared o tal vez en el aire,*
*unos sin haber empezado a vivir.*

*Pero todos se van con los pies atados,*
*unos por el camino que hicieron,*
*otros por el que no hicieron*
*y todos por el que nunca haran.*

Each one goes as best they can,
some with their chests open,
others with only one hand,
some with the identity card in their pocket,
others in the soul,
some with the moon screwed in the blood
and others without blood, nor moon, nor memories.

Each one goes even if they can't,
some with love between their teeth,
others changing their skin,
some with life and death,
others with death and life,
some with their hand on their shoulder
and others with it on the shoulder of another.

Each one goes because they're going,
some with someone sleepless between their eyebrows,
others without having crossed paths with anyone,
some through the door that seemingly opens onto the road,
others through a door drawn on the wall or perhaps in the air,
some without having begun to live
and others without having begun to live.

But everyone leaves with their feet tied,
some along the path they took,
others for what they did not do
and all for which they will never do.

*Vertical Poetry, II.22, 1963*


*La ultima luz se suelda siempre a la mano.*
*Es un fruto,*
*un cuerpo ya completo.*
*Si despues de ella*
*fuera posible aun otro regreso,*
*todo el cuerpo veria.*
*La luz del agua es el agua,*
*la de la sombra, la sombra,*
*y la de un pie, el otro pie.*

The last light is always soldered by hand.
It is a fruit,
an already complete body.
Yes after her
if another return was possible,
the whole body would see.
The light of the water is the water,
the one with the shadow, the shadow,
and that of one foot, the other foot.

*Vertical Poetry, II.23, 1963*

*Despues de media vida o quiza toda,*
*pocas cosas resisten:*
*el lugar donde las paralelas tiemblan,*
*la noche en que un amor muerto vuelve a estar vivo,*
*una instancia que no es la luz, la sombra*
      *ni sus gradaciones intermedias,*
*un sitio que no es el todo menos los otros,*
*ciertas introducciones hacia afuera.*

*Formas de fidelidades que ignoramos,*
*solo en ellas es posible*
*posteaar un poco la imposibilidad de todo.*

After half a life or maybe all of it,
few things resist:
the place where the parallels tremble,
the night when a dead love is alive again,
an instance that is not light, shadow
          or their intermediate gradations,
a place that is not everything except the others,
certain outward introductions.

Forms of fidelity that we ignore,
only in them is it possible
to postpone a little the impossibility of everything.

*Vertical Poetry, II, 26, 1963*


*Un largo tunel se me acerca a la boca*
*y me baja la voz,*
*este amillo que no termina nunca de cerrarse.*

*He buscado en vano una palabra*
*que sirva como dedo del anillo,*
*ahora mucho mas cerca.*

*Si este tunel fuese suficientemente largo,*
*si retornara cada vez de su extremo,*
*el mismo seria el dedo.*

*Solo uando haya dedo se cerrara el anillo.*

A long tunnel approaches my mouth
and my voice drops,
this ring that never ends closing.

I have searched in vain for a word
that serves as a ring finger,
now much closer.

If this tunnel were long enough,
if it returned every time from its extreme,
the same would be the finger.

Only when there is a finger will the ring close.

*Vertical Poetry, III.9, 1965*


*Alguna vez juego alcanzarme.*
*Corro con el que fui*
*y con el que sere*
*la carrera del que soy.*

*Y alguna vez juego a pasarme*
*Corro entonces quiza*
*la carrera del que no soy.*

*Pero hay todavia otra Carrera*
*en la que jugare a hacerme pasar*
*Y esa sera la carrera verdadera.*

Sometimes I play catch up.
I run with the one I was
and with whom I will be
in the race of what I am.

And sometimes I play I pass myself.
Then maybe I run
the race of which I am not.

But there is yet another race
in which I play that I am passed
and that will be the true race.

*La vida dibuja un arbol*
*y la muerte dibuja otro*
*La vida dibuja un nido*
*y la muerte lo copia.*
*La vida dibuja un pajaro*
*para que habite el nido*
*y la muerte de inmediato*
*dibuja otro pajaro.*

*Una mano que no dibuja nada*
*se pasea entre todos los dibujos*
*y cada tanto cambia uno de sitio.*
*Por ejemplo:*
*el pajaro de la vida*
*ocupa el nida de la muerte*
*sobre el arbol dibujado por la vida.*

*Otras veces*
*la mano que no dibuja nada*
*borra un dibujo de la serie.*
*Por ejemplo:*
*el arbol de la muerte*
*sostiene el nido de la muerte,*
*pero no lo ocupa ningun parajo.*

Life draws a tree
and death draws another.
Life draws a nest
and death copies it.
Life draws a bird
to inhabit the nest
and death immediately
draws another bird.

A hand that does not draw anything
walks through all the drawings
and from time to time one changes places.
For example:
the bird of life
occupies the nest of death
on the tree drawn by life.

Other times
the hand that does not draw anything
deletes a drawing from the series.
For example:
the tree of death
holds the nest of death,
but no bird occupies it.

*Y otras veces
la mano que no dibuja nada
se convierte a si misma
en imagen sobrante,
con figura de pajaro,
con figura de arbol,
con figura de nido.
Y entonces, solo entonces,
no falta ni sobra nada.
Por ejemplo:
dos parajaros
ocupan el nido de la vida
sobre el arbol de la muerte.*

*O el arbol de la vida
sostiene dos nidos
en los que habita un soilo pajaro.*

*O un parjaro unico
habita un solo nido
sobre el arbol de la vida
y el arbol de la muerte.*

And other times
the hand that does not draw anything
converts itself
into a leftover image,
with a figure of a bird,
with a figure of a tree,
with a figure of a nest.
And then, only then,
nothing is missing or left over.
For example:
two birds
occupy the nest of life
on the tree of death.

Or the tree of life
holds two nests
in which a single bird lives.

Or a unique bird
inhabits a single nest
on the tree of life
and the tree of death.

*Vertical Poetry, IV.2, 1969*


*Una mosca anda cabeza abajo por el techo,*
*un hombre anda cabeza abajo por la calle*
*y algun dios anda cabeza abajo por la nada.*

*Tan solo tu no andas esta tarde,*
*a menos que las ausencias puras*
*inventen otra forma de andar que no sabemos:*
*andar cabeza arriba.*

*Exploraremos el encuentro del amor y la piedra,*
*el viaje de la mano a su duelo,*
*la playa de banderas con que suena la sangre,*
*la fiesta de ser hombre cuando el hombre despierta*
*y se cae en el hombre,*
*la fabula que se convierte en nino,*
*la mujer necessaria para amar lo que amamos*
*y hasta lo que no amamos.*
*Y exploraremos tambien el espacio vacio*
*que dejaste en tu poema,*
*el espacio vacio que dejaste en cada palabra*
*y hasta en tu propria tumba*
*para alzar el futuro.*

*Alli te encontraremos*
*y juntos echareos a andar cabeza arriba.*


*(A Paul Eluard)*

A fly walks upside down on the ceiling,
a man walks head down along the street
and some god walks head down through nothing.

Only you are not walking this afternoon,
unless pure absences
invent another way of walking that we don't know:
walking head up.

Let's explore the meeting of love and stone,
the journey hand in hand to your grief,
the beach of flags with which the blood rings,
the celebration of being a man when the man wakes up
and falls into becoming a man,
the fable that becomes a child,
the woman necessary to love what we love
and even what we don't love.
And we will also explore the empty space
        that you left in your poem,
the empty space you left in each word
and even in your own grave
to lift the future.

We will find you there
and together you will start walking head up.

*(To Paul Eluard)*

*Vertical Poetry, IV.3, 1969*

*En alguna parte hay un hombre*
*que transpira pensamiento.*
*Sobre su piel se dibujan*
*los contornos humedos de una piel mas fina,*
*la estela de una navegacion sin nave.*

*Cuando ese hombre piensa luz, ilumina,*
*cuando piensa muerte, se alisa,*
*cuando recuerda a alguien, adquiere sus ragos,*
*cuando cae en si mismo, se oscurece como un pozo.*

*En el se ve el color de los pensamientos nocturnos*
*y se aprende que ningun pensamiento carece*
*de su noche y su dia.*
*Y tambien que hay colores y pensamientos*
*que no nacen de dia ni de noche,*
*sino tan solo cuando crece un poco mad el olvido.*

*Ese hombre tiene la porosidad de una tierra mas viva*
*y a veces, cuando suena, toma aspecto de fuego.*
*salpicaduras de una llama que se alimenta con llama,*
*retorcimientos de bosque calcinado.*

*A ese hombre se le puede ver el amor,*
*pero eso tan solo quien lo encuentre y lo ame.*
*Y tambien se podria ver en su carne a dios,*
*pero solo despues de dejar de ver todo el resto.*

*(A Octavio Paz)*

Somewhere there is a man
that sweats thought.
On his skin they are drawn
the moist contours of a thinner skin,
the wake of a navigation without a ship.

When that man thinks light, he is illumined,
when he thinks of death, he smoothes himself out,
when he remembers someone, he takes on their features,
when he falls into himself, he becomes dark like a well.

In him you can see the color of night thoughts
and you learn that no thought is lacking
of his night and his day.
And also that there are colors and thoughts
that are not born during the day or at night,
but only when forgetfulness grows a little more.

That man is porous, an earth that is more alive
and sometimes, when it rings, takes the appearance of fire.
splashes of a flame that is fed with flame,
twists of charred forest.

You can see the love in that man,
but that is only for those who find him and love him.
And you could also see God in his flesh,
but only after you stop seeing everything else.

*(To Octavio Paz)*

*Vertical Poetry, IV.4, 1969*


*Estoy despierto.*
*Me duermo.*
*Sueno que estoy despierto.*
*Sueno que me duermo.*
*Sueno que sueno.*

*Sueno que sueno*
*que estoy despierto.*
*Sueno que sueno*
*que me duermo.*
*Sueno que sueno*
*que sueno.*

*Estoy despierto.*

I'm awake.
I'm asleep.
I dream that I am awake.
I dream that I fall asleep.
I dream that I dream.

I dream that I dream
I'm awake.
I dream that I dream
I fall asleep.
I dream that I dream
that I dream.

I'm awake.

*Vertical Poetry, IV.5, 1969*

*Un muro, una cancion*
*y un como barniz de duende*
*para que la cancion descanse sobre el muro.*
*Del otro lado, un hombre.*
*No ha levantado el muro*
*ni canta la cancion,*
*ni siquiera la eschucha.*
*Pero el aire barniz cava en su sombra un circulo*
*en donde la cancion es justamente el centro.*

*El hombre esta agachado*
*(tal vez lo estuvo siempre).*
*El muro baja entonces*
*y le sube los ojos.*

*Una cancion*
*(no importa quien la cante),*
*un muro*
*(no importa quien lo ha hecho)*
*y un aire liso y vivo*
*(no importa adonde vaya).*

*Si el hombre no existiera,*
*ellos lo habrian creado.*

A wall, a song
and an air like a gloss of lacquer,
so that the song rests on the wall.
On the other side, a man.
He has not raised the wall
nor sings the song,
he doesn't even listen to it.
But the lacquered air digs in its shadow a circle
where the song is precisely in the center.

The man is crouched
(maybe he always was).
The wall goes down then
and he raises his eyes.

A song
(it doesn't matter who sings it),
a wall
(it doesn't matter who raised it)
and a smooth and lively air
(no matter where you go).

If the man did not exist,
they would have created him.

*Vertical Poetry, IV.6, 1969*

*Llueve sobre el pensamiento.*

*Y el pensamiento llueve sobre el mundo*
*como los restos de una diezmada red*
*cuyas mallas no aciertan a encontrarse.*

*Llueve adentro del pensamiento.*

*Y el pensamiento rebalsa y llueve adentro del mundo,*
*colmando desde el centro todos los recipientes,*
*hasta los mas guardado y sellados.*

*Llueve bajo el pensamiento.*

*Y el pensamiento llueve bajo el mundo,*
*borrando los cimientos de las cosas,*
*para fundar de nuevo la habitacion del hombre y de la vida.*

*Llueve sin el pensamiento.*

*Y el pensamiento*
*sigue lloviendo aun sin el mundo,*
*sigue lloviendo sin la lluvia,*
*sigue lloviendo.*

It rains onto thought.

And thought rains over the world
like the remains of a decimated net
whose meshes cannot be found.

It rains inside thought.

And thought overflows and rains inside the world,
filling all the containers from the center,
even the most guarded and sealed ones.

It rains under thought.

And the thought rains under the world,
erasing the foundations of things,
to found again the habitation of man and life.

It rains without thought.

And thought
keeps raining even without the world,
keeps raining without the rain,
keeps raining.

*Vertical Poetry, IV, 7, 1969*


*Si conocieram0s el punto*
*donde va a romperse algo,*
*donde se cortara el hilo do los besos,*
*donde una mirada dejara de encontrarse con otra mirada,*
*donde el corazon saltara hacia otro sitio,*
*podriamos poner otro punto sobre ese punto*
*o por lo menos acompanarlo al romperse.*

*Si conocieramos el punto*
*donde algo va a fundirse con algo,*
*donde el desierto se encontrara con la lluvia,*
*donde el abrazo se tocara con la vida,*
*donde mi muerte se aproximara a la tuya,*
*podriamos desenvolver ese punto como una serpentina*
*o por lo menos cantarlo hasta morirnos.*

*Si concieramos el punto*
*donde algo sera siempre ese algo,*
*donde el hueso no olivdara a la carne,*
*donde la fuente es madre de otra fuente,*
*donde el pasado dejar solo ese punto y borrar todos los otros*
*o guardarlo por lo menos en un lugar mas seguro.*

*(A Laura)*

If we knew the point
where something is going to break,
where the thread of kisses will be cut,
where one look would stop meeting another look,
where the heart will jump to another place,
we could put another point on that point.
or at least accompany it when it breaks.

If we knew the point
where something is going to merge with something,
where the desert met the rain,
where the hug touched life,
where my death would approach yours,
we could unwrap that song like a streamer
or at least sing it until we die.

If we knew the point
where something will always be that something,
where the bone will not forget the flesh,
where the source is the mother of another source,
where the past leaves only that point and erases all the others
or store it at least in a safer place.

(*To Laura*)

*Vertical Poetry, V.1, 1974*

*En la raiz de la palabra*
*juegan various amores,*
*pero tambien un sombrio color*
*parcido a las banderas de una batalla perdida.*

*Hablar es mivir de otra manera,*
*pero tambien morir de otra manera,*
*como si vivir fuera morir,*
*como si morir fuera vivir.*

*En la raiz de la palabra*
*todo amor va mas alla de los que ama,*
*pero vuelve con una flor imprudentenmente oscura*
*y reconoce que no puede ir mas alla.*

*Es por eso que despues de la palabra*
*en su raiz se abre un espacio sin pasion ni sarcasmo,*
*un espacio desde el cual puende crecer ya liberimente*
*la ausencia mas humana que habita en el hombre.*

At the root of the word
various loves play,
but also a somber color
similar to the flags of a lost battle.

To speak is to live in another way,
but also die in another way,
as if living were dying,
as if dying was living.

At the root of the word
all love goes beyond those it loves,
but returns with a recklessly dark flower
and recognizes that it cannot go any further.

That is why after the word, at its root,
a space opens up without passion or sarcasm,
a space from which the most human absence
that inhabits man can grow freely.

*Lo vacio del dia
se condensa en un punto
que cae como una gota
en el rio.*

*Lo lleno del dia
se condensa en un minimo orificio
que aspira aquella gota
del rio.*

*Desde que lleno a que vacio
desde que vacio a que lleno
corre el rio.*

The emptiness of the day,
condensing into a point,
falls like a drop
in the river.

The fullness of the day
condenses into a minimal hole
sucking that drop
out of its rush.

From full to empty,
from empty to full
the river runs.

*Vertical Poetry, V.3, 1974*


*El ojo traza en el techo blanco
una pequena raya negra.
El techo asume la ilusion del ojo
y se vuelve negro.
La raya se borra entonces
y el ojo se cierra.*

*Asi nace la soledad.*

The eye traces on the white ceiling
a small black stripe.
The ceiling assumes the illusion of the eye
and it turns black.
The line is then erased
and the eye closes.

This is how loneliness is born.

*Vertical Poetry, VI.4, 1974*

*La campana esta llena de viento,*
*aunque no suene.*
*El pajaro esta lleno de vuelo,*
*aunque este quieto.*
*El cielo esta lleno nubes,*
*aunque este solo.*
*La palabra esta llena de voz,*
*aunque nadie la diga.*
*Toda cosa esta llena de fugas,*
*aunque no hay caminos.*

*Todas las cosas huyen*
*hacia su presencia.*

The bell is full of wind,
although it doesn't sound.
The bird is full of flight,
although it is still.
The sky is full of clouds,
although it is alone.
The word is full of voice,
although no one says it.
Everything is full of flights,
although there are no roads.

All things flee
towards its presence.

*Vertical Poetry, VI.5, 1974*


*El relampago de la belleza*
*crea la eternidad en el reves del ojo.*

*El relampago del amor*
*crea la eternidad en la espalda del olvido.*

*El relampago de la vida*
*cra la eternidad en la otra cara de la muerte.*

*El relampago del instante*
*crea la eternidad del otro lado del tiempo.*

*Toda luz ilumina.*
*Y hasta quiza deslumbra.*
*Pero la claridad esta en el reverso de la luz.*

The lightning of beauty
creates eternity in the back of the eye.

The lightning of love
creates eternity on the back of forgetfulness.

The lightning of living
creates eternity on the other side of death.

The lightning of the moment
creates eternity on the other side of time.

Every light illuminates.
And maybe it even dazzles.
But clarity resides on the other side of light.

*Vertical Poetry, 7.1, 1982*


*Usar la propia mano como almohada.*
*El cielo lo hace con sus nubes,*
*la tierra con sus terrones*
*y el arbol que cae*
*con su propio follaje.*

*Solo asi puede escucharse*
*la cancion sin distancia,*
*la cancion que no entra en el oido*
*porque esta en el oido,*
*la unica cancion que no se repite.*

*Todo hombre necesita*
*una cancion intraducible.*

Use your own hand as a pillow.
Sky does it with its clouds,
earth with its clods
and the tree that falls
with its own foliage.

Only then can the song
without distance be heard,
the song that never enters the ear
because it's already in the ear,
the only song that is not repeated.

All people need
an untranslatable song.

*Desde abajo de todo*
*brota la voz de una campana.*
*No sirve para llamar al templo,*
*ni para anunciar la primavera,*
*ni para acompanar a un muerto.*
*Solo sirve para sonar*
*como lo haria un hombre*
*con los ojos abiertos*
*si fuera una campana.*
*Solo sirve*
*para rodear a los pajaros perdidos*
*con un aire mas sonoro.*
*Solo sirve*
*para que dure el canto*
*que no va a ninguna parte.*

*Una simple campana*
*que suena desde abajo*
*como un movimiento natural,*
*sin que nadie la agite,*
*sin que nadie la oiga,*
*como si el fondo de todo*
*no fuera otra cosa*
*que el desinteresado taner de una campana.*

From below everything
sounds the voice of a bell.
It doesn't serve as a call to temple,
not even to announce spring,
not even to accompany a dead person.
It only serves to sound
as a man would do
with his eyes open
if he were a bell.
It only works
to surround the lost birds
with a more sonorous air.
It only works
so that the song lasts
that's not going anywhere.

A simple bell
that sounds from below
like a natural movement,
without anyone shaking it;
without anyone hearing it
as if at the bottom of everything
there wasn't anything else than
a bell ringing in total detachment.

*Vertical Poetry, VII.17, 1982*

*Todo silencio es un espacio magico,*
*con un rito escondido,*
*la matriz de una palabra convocatoria*
*y un imprescindible detalle de antisilencio.*

*El rito escondido puede ser por ejemplo*
*una muerte en invierno,*
*la palaba en gestacion*
*puede ser sencillamente la palabra olvido*
*y el detalle de antisilencio*
*puede ser el golpe de unos terrones contra la tierra.*

*O el rito la oscilacion de una ternura en la noche,*
*la palabra, un nombre que se ahogo,*
*y el infaltable detalle de antisilencio*
*un poco de agua que se deslizza por el sueno del mundo.*

*O el rito puede ser la soledad de un poema,*
*la palabra el signo que todo poema oculta*
*y el punto de antisilencio*
*el sonido de la mano que llama desde adentro del poema.*

*El silencio es un templo*
*que no necesita dios.*

All silence is a magical space,
with a hidden rite,
the matrix of a word summons
and an essential detail of anti-silence.

The hidden rite can be for example
a death in winter,
the word in gestation
could simply be the word oblivion
and the detail of anti-silence
could be the impact of some clods against the earth.

Or the rite the swing of a tenderness in the night,
the word, a name that was drowned,
and the inevitable detail of anti-silence
a little water that slides through the dream of the world.

Or the rite can be the loneliness of a poem,
the word the sign that every poem hides
and the point of anti-silence
the sound of the hand calling from within the poem.

Silence is a temple
that does not need god.

*Vertical Poetry, VIII, 1984*

*Hay que empezar a abandonar cada tanto la escritura*
*y aprender a convivir con la pagina en blanco,*
*con su llanura desmasiado lisa,*
*con su horizonte demansiado abierto.*

*Hay que dejar en suspenso nuestras figuraciones*
*para aproximarnos a nuestras transfiguraciones*
*y dialogar con ellas en el extremo del blanco,*
*sin tener siquiera la letra como testigo.*

You have to start abandoning writing from time to time
and learn to live with the blank page,
with its too smooth plainness,
with its horizon too open.

We must leave our imaginations in suspense
to approach our transfigurations
and dialogue with them at the end of the target,
without even having the handwriting as a witness.

*Vertical Poetry, IX.1, 1988*


*Morir, pero lejos.*
*No aqui,*
*donde todo es una aviesa*
*conspiracion de la vida,*
*hasta las otras muertes.*

*Morir lejos.*
*No aqui,*
*donde morir es ya una traicion,*
*mas traicion que en otra parte.*

*Morir lejos.*
*No aqui,*
*donde la soledad descansa a ratos*
*como si fuera un animal tendido,*
*olvidando su espuela de locura.*

*Morir lejos.*
*No aqui,*
*donde cada uno se duerma*
*siempre en el mismo sitio,*
*aunque despierte siempre en otro.*

*Morir lejos.*
*No aqui.*
*Morir donde nadie nos espere,*
*donde haya lugar para morir.*

To die, but far away.
Not here,
where everything is evil
conspiracy of life,
until the other deaths.

To die far away.
Not here,
where dying is already a betrayal,
more traction than elsewhere.

To die far away.
Not here,
where loneliness rests at times
as if it were a lying animal,
forgetting its spur of madness.

To die far away.
Not here,
where everyone falls asleep
always in the same place,
although always wakes up in another.

To die far away.
Not here.
To die where no one expects us,
where there is a place to die.

*Vertical Poetry, IX.5, 1988*

*Se ha perdido una nota.*
*No sabemos el compas ni la escala,*
*pero la obra se descompone bacia el poniente*
*como un flecha rozada al pasar por una pluma.*

*Se ha extraviado una linea.*
*No sabemos la figura o el cuadro,*
*pero la imagen se acorrala contra un borde*
*como una fiesta en cuyo centro cae un fruto negro.*

*Se ha borrado un matiz.*
*No sabemos en que zona o que mundo,*
*pero ese casi nada irreparable*
*lo hiere todo para siempre.*


*—Roberto Juarroz*

A note has been lost.
We do not know the compass or the scale,
but the work decomposes towards the west
like an arrow grazed as it passes through a feather.

A line has been lost.
We don't know the figure or the picture,
but the image is cornered against an edge
like a celebration in the center of which a black fruit falls.

A nuance has been erased.
We don't know in what area or what world,
but that almost nothing irreparable
hurts everything forever.

*Decima.44*

*Me doy vuelta hacia tu lado,*
*En el lecho la vida,*
*y encuentro que estas hecha de imposible.*

*Me vuelvo entonces hacia mi*
*y hallo la misma cosa.*

*Es por eso*
*que aunque amemos lo posible,*
*terminaremos por encerrarlo en una caja,*
*para que no estorbe mas a este imposible*
*sin el cual no podemos seguir juntos.*

*(para Laura otra vez, mientras nos acercamos)*

Tenth.44


I turn to your side,
in bed or life,
and I find that you are made of what is impossible.

I then turn towards myself
and find the same thing.

That is why
although we love the possible,
we will end up locking it in a box,
so that it no longer hinders this impossible thing
without which we cannot remain together.

*(to Larua again, as we become closer)*

*Undecmia.I.10 (from Eleventh Vertical Poetry)*

*Sone un manuscrito*
*Cuyas lineas se borraban una a una.*
*Sone tambien a quienes lo escribian*
*—uno era yo—*
*y tambien se borraban uno a uno.*

*Al despertar*
*no quedaba ya nadie.*
*Y habia una unica linea,*
*que tambien comenaba a borrarse.*
*Esa linea decia:*
*Solo dios puede salvar de dios.*

**Eleventh.I.10 (from Eleventh Vertical Poetry)**


I dreamed there was a manuscript
whose lines were erased one by one.
I dreamed also of those who wrote them
—one of them was me—
and they were also erased one by one.

When I woke
there was no one left.
And there was a single line,
which was also beginning to fade.
That line said:
Only God can save you from God.

*Undecima.II.15*


*Un zumbido de fondo*
*acusa la presencia de las cosas.*
*Necesitamos la palabra y el viento*
*para poder soportarlo.*

*Un zumbido de fondo*
*denuncia la ausencia de las cosas.*
*Necesitamos inventar otra memoria*
*para no enloquecer.*

*Un zumbido de fondo*
*anuncia que no hay nada*
*que no pueda existir.*
*Necesitamos un silencio doblado de silencio*
*para aceptar que todo exisite.*

*Un zumbido fondo*
*subraya el frio de la muerte.*
*Necesitamos la suma de todos los cantos*
*y el resumen de todos los amores*
*para poder aplacar ese zumbido.*

*O una tarde caulquiera,*
*sin mas condicion que su abertura,*
*vendra un pajaro a posarse en el aire*
*como si el aire fuera otra rama.*
*Y entonces cesaran todos los zumbidos.*

Eleventh.11.15


A hum in the background
accuses the presence of things.
We need the word and the wind
to be able to endure it.

A hum in the background
denounces the absence of things.
We need to invent another memory
so as not to go crazy.

A hum in the background
announces that there is nothing
that cannot exist.
We need a silence doubled from silence
to accept that everything exists.

A background hum
underlines the cold of death.
We need the sum of all the songs
and the summary of all the loves
to be able to calm that buzz.

Or any given afternoon,
with no other condition than its opening,
a bird will come to perch in the air
as if the air were another branch.
And then all the humming will stop.

*Undecima.III.8 (from Eleventh Vertical Poetry, 1988)*


Las palabras no son talismanes.
Pero cualquier cosa puede
transmutarse en poesia
si la toca la palabra indicada.

No es asunto de magia ni de alquimia.
Se trata de pensar de otro modo las cosas,
palparlas de otro modo,
abandonar a las palabras que las cantan,
las palabras que las levantan el viento
como clavos ardiendo en el asombro.

Estacas convertidas en estrellas,
zapatos para calzar crucifixiones,
cegueras abiertas en la espalda del dia,
visiones reservadas para volver a despertar,
ternuras que se postergan para salvar el amor.

Se trata solamente de crear otra voz:
la voz ausente adentro de las cosas.

**Eleventh.III.8 (from Eleventh Vertical Poetry, 1988)**

Words are not talismans.
But anything can be
transmuted into poetry
if the right word touches it.

It is not a matter of magic or alchemy.
It is about thinking about things differently,
feeling them differently,
abandon the words that sing them,
the words that lift them in the wind
like burning nails in amazement.

Stakes turned into stars,
shoes to wear crucifixions,
open blindnesses on the back of the day,
visions reserved to reawaken,
tendernesses that are postponed to save love.

It is just about creating another voice:
the absent voice inside things.

*Undecima.IV.2 (from Eleventh Vertical Poetry, 1988)*

*For W. S. Merwin*

*Los ojos dormidos buscan otro color.*
*Alguien apago los colores*
*como apaga las lamparas.*
*El territorio de los ojos*
*se convirtio en desierto.*

*Despertar debiera ser*
*despertar hacia adentro*
*y encontrar en el fondo*
*ese nuevo atributo,*
*tal vez el duplicado de reserva*
*de todos los colores.*
*Sin embargo, las lamparas*

*O quiza la identidad insolita*
*del que puede encenderlos de nuevo,*
*como quien enciende las lamparas,*
*aunque a veces las cubra.*

*Sin embargo, las lamparas*
*Tambien se encienden solas.*
*Tal vez sea eso lo que buscan*
*los ojos que se duremen.*

Eleventh.IV.2 (from Eleventh Vertical Poetry, 1988)



Sleeping eyes look for another color.
Someone turned off the color
like they turn off the lamps.
The territory of the eyes
itself became a desert.

Waking up should be
awaking inwardly
and finding deep down
that new attribute,
perhaps the reserve duplicate
of all the colors.

Or perhaps the unusual identity
of the one who can turn them on again,
like someone who turns on the lamps,
although sometimes they cover them.

However, the lamps
also turn on by themselves.
Maybe that's what the eyes are looking for
when they fall asleep.

*Por un instante se encontraron*
*las miradas de los vivos*
*y las miradas de los muertos*
*y no chocaron como punos*
*ni mellaron el filo del contacto*
*ni hubo tampoco ningun parpado o eclipse*
*que crensurara la peligrosa entrevision.*

*Las miradas de los vivos y los muertos*
*se encontraron nada mas que un instante*
*para excavar en el sitio del encuentro*
*un regazo menos asperto,*
*un espacio no comprometido,*
*una zona al margen de la vida y las muerte.*

For a moment they met
the looks of the living
and the looks of the dead.
And they didn't collide like fists,
nor did they blunt the edge of contact,
nor was there any eyelid or eclipse
that would censor the dangerous glimpse.

The looks of the living and the dead
they met for nothing more than a moment
to excavate at the meeting site
a less rough lap,
an uncommitted space,
an area on the margins of life and death.

# ACKNOWLEDGEMENTS

Six translations from the Spanish of Roberto Juarroz were initially featured in *Ezra: An Online Journal of Translation*, in the Winter 2025 Issue. They include:

*"A day will come," "After half a life or maybe all of it," "Each one goes as best they can," "It shouldn't be possible," "The last light is always soldered by hand," "Sometimes I play catch up."*

The essay, *"Untranslatable Song: The Vertical Poetry of Roberto Juarroz,"* used here as the introduction to this collection, was initially featured in *Your Impossible Voice,* January 2024.

*"Going up is nothing more," "If we knew the point," "Use your own hand as a pillow,"* and *"You have to start abandoning writing from time to time"* also were initially published in Your Impossible Voice, embedded within the essay, and are the first appearances of each of these specific translations.

I also specifically offer my gratitude to both Peter Thompson, editor of *Ezra: An Online Journal of Translation* and Keith Powell, editor of Your Impossible Voice, for their not only publishing these translations of the work of Robert Juarroz but also for their consistent support of my work over the years.

Thanks to the editors of The Acentos Review who published the following translations of Roberto Juarroz online: *"Vertical Poetry I. 22, 1958," "Vertical Poetry I. 4, 1958," Vertical Poetry VI. 4, 1974."*

*"Vertical Poetry, II.26, 1963," "Vertical Poetry, IV.1, 1969," "Vertical Poetry, IV.2, 1969,"* and *"Vertical Poetry, IV.3, 1969"* were featured in La Piccioletta Barca, based at Cambridge University in the United Kingdom, on 2 August 2024.

## PUBLICATIONS

Aperture (Kelsay Books, 2025)
Discovering What to Say (Bainbridge Island Press, 2025)
If You're the Dreamer, I'm the Dream: Selected Translations
    from Rilke's Book of Hours (Finishing Line Press, 2025)
L'Allegria: Giuseppe Ungaretti (Shanti Arts Publishing, 2023)
A Writer's Statements on Beauty: New & Selected Essays &
    Reviews (Shanti Arts Publishing, 2022)
Taking Residence (Shanti Arts Publishing, 2021)
Awakening & Visitation (Shanti Arts Publishing, 2020)
Evanescence: Selected Poems (Shanti Arts Publishing, 2020)
A Bird Who Seems to Know Me: Poems Regarding
    Birds & Nature (Ex Ophidia Press, 2019)
The Bees of the Invisible (Shanti Arts Publishing, 2019)
On Beauty: Essays, Reviews, Fiction,
    and Plays (Adelaide Books, 2018)
Singing for Nothing: Selected Nonfiction
    as Literary Memoir (Operating System, 2018)
The Map of Eternity (Shanti Arts Publishing, 2018)
Candling the Eggs (Shanti Arts Publishing, 2017)
The View of the River (Kelsay Books, 2017)
The Windbreak Pine (Snapshot Press, 2016)
The Daodejing: An Interpretation, with David Breeden
    and Steven Schroeder (Lamar University Literary Press, 2015)
Invocation (Lamar University Literary Press, 2015)
Velocity (Virtual Artists Collective, 2013)
Blessing and Homage (Timberline Press, 2012)
Huang Po and the Dimensions
    of Love (Southern Illinois University Press, 2012)
Winding Paths Worn through Grass (Virtual Artists Collective, 2012)
Luminous Dream (FutureCycle Press, 2010)
Mount Toby Poems (Timberline Press, 2009)
The Silence Between Us (Brooks Books, 2005)
The White Rose (Timberline Press, 2000))
The New Life (Plinth Books, 1998)
The Mown Meadow (Los Hombres Press, 1996)
For the Dance (Adastra Press, 1991)

# Wally Swist

**W**ally Swist's books include *Huang Po* and the *Dimensions of Love* (Southern Illinois University Press, 2012); *The Daodejing: A New Interpretation*, with David Breeden and Steven Schroeder (Lamar University Literary Press, 2015); and the winner of the ***2018 Ex Ophidia Press Poetry Prize*** for his book, *A Bird Who Seems to Know Me: Poems Regarding Birds & Nature.*

His forthcoming books include *The Map of Eternity* (Shanti Arts, LLC, 2018), *Singing for Nothing: Selected Nonfiction as Literary Memoir* (The Operating System, 2018), and *On Beauty: Essays, Reviews, Fiction, and Plays* (Adelaide Books, 2018).

His poems and prose have appeared in *Adelaide Literary Journal*; *The American Book Review*; *Appalachia Journal*; *Arts: The Arts in Theological and Religious Studies*; *Chiron Review*, *Crab Orchard Review*; *The Galway Review* (Ireland); *North American Review*; *Still Point Arts Quarterly*; and *Transference: A Literary Journal Featuring the Art and Process of Translation.*